# Sew
# Outdoor
# Living

Debbie Shore

**Brighten up your garden with
22 colourful projects**

D0125501

SEARCH PRESS

# Contents

*Pompom Tablecloth,*
*page 16*

*Reverse Appliqué Heart Placemat,*
*page 18*

*Plant Pot Covers,*
*page 22*

*Bunting in a Bag,*
*page 24*

*Frilled Chair Pillow,*
*page 28*

*Patchwork Picnic Mat,*
*page 32*

*Buttoned Pillow,*
*page 36*

*Teepee,*
*page 40*

# Introduction

After spending many hours in the garden during a particularly warm summer, I thought how wonderful it would be to furnish the outdoor living area with the same consideration I give to my house: with comfortable seating areas to relax in and well-dressed tables for al fresco dining. I take my work outdoors as often as I can – I'm fortunate to live in the quiet Lincolnshire countryside, which is the perfect environment for sewing, sketching, writing and, of course, entertaining!

Whether your outdoor area is large enough to throw garden parties or just big enough for a table and chairs, I'm sure you'll find ideas and inspiration here for making your sunny space both comfortable and stylish.

Debbie
x

# 10 tips for the complete beginner

1  Start with a simple project such as the Pompom Tablecloth (page 16) or Knotted Bolster Pillow (page 46). As your skills grow you'll feel confident to tackle slightly more advanced projects like the Teepee (page 40) or Tic Tac Toe set (page 66).

2  Make up your project in inexpensive fabric first. That way if things go wrong, you're not wasting anything but time!

3  As the saying goes, measure twice cut once! Stitches can be unpicked but if you don't cut the right size there's little you can do.

4  Reverse a couple of stitches at the start and end of your sewing line. Some machines have a 'fix' stitch that puts three or four tiny stitches close together. This will stop the stitches coming undone.

5  Cut your fabric pieces on the grain – this means that the weave of the fabric sits vertically and horizontally; if you cut at an angle – known as 'on the bias' – your fabric could twist out of shape.

6  To help you sew in a straight line and create even seam allowances, place a strip of masking tape over the bed of your sewing machine as a guide for your fabric (an elastic band around the free arm works well too). Measure from the needle 5mm (¼in) to the right and place your tape at this point. Throughout the book, seam allowances are 5mm (¼in) unless otherwise stated.

7  Topstitching – a visible line of stitching – can be a bit daunting, so sew slowly. If you're not very confident, use a thread that matches your fabric so that it doesn't stand out too much.

8  Pin at right angles to the edge of your fabric. You'll find the layers don't slip and, although you should be taking out your pins as you sew, if the needle accidentally hits a pin there is less chance of either breaking.

9  Change your sewing-machine needle regularly. It is recommended you put a new needle in after every eight hours of sewing – you'll notice a difference to the stitches and even the sound of your machine! It's always good form when you change the needle to take off the needle plate and clean out any lint. (Take a look at your manufacturer's instructions.)

10  Relax! Sewing is fun! Don't worry if things go a bit wrong – put your work down and come back to it the next day. It won't seem half as bad as you first thought!

# Materials & tools

## Fabrics

Choose the same kind of fabrics for the pillow covers and table dressings as you would for indoor projects; you'll bring these items inside in bad weather, and some may need to be laundered. I use a quality, woven cotton for most of my projects: pre-wash this to avoid shrinkage. Projects such as the Bean Bag Stool (see page 50) and Teepee (see page 40) will need slightly stronger fabric, such as canvas, ticking or denim – plain or patterned, the choice is yours! These won't need to be pre-washed as spot cleaning is the best option for larger projects.

## Threads

Try to use the same composition as your fabric: cotton for cotton, polyester for man-made, silk for silk. Always use a good-quality thread – your seams will be stronger and they'll produce less lint, which can build up inside your machine.

## Wadding/batting

This is the layer of padding put between two pieces of fabric to give structure, warmth and a luxurious feel to a project. It can be made from many different fibres: cotton, polyester, silk, wool or bamboo, to name a few, and sometimes several fibres are mixed together. The big decision is choosing a type. A lot depends on what you're using it for, and whether the item will be washed. I like natural, organic, untreated fibres for breathability and softness, and prefer types that are fire-retardant.

The 'loft' refers to the thickness of the wadding/batting: the higher the loft the thicker the wadding/batting. Low loft is preferred for quilting.

Fusible fleece gives structure and is simply ironed onto the wrong side of your fabric – some types contain thermal threads, making them perfect for insulation or heat protection.

## Sewing machine

I always recommend a computerized machine. They're simple to use, and have a comprehensive range of stitches that are automatically set to the required stitch width, length and tension. Make sure your machine comes with a guarantee and support. The projects in this book can be made with quite a basic machine, so don't think you have to spend a lot of money on one.

# Cutting your fabric

### ROTARY CUTTER, RULER AND MAT

Well worth the investment, these tools will help you measure and cut accurately and quickly. The bigger the better! The most-used size of rotary cutter is 45mm (1¾in); use with a long acrylic ruler and a self-healing cutting mat to ensure the most accurate straight-line cutting.

### SHEARS

Shears aren't just for dressmaking; they have angled blades to help keep your fabric flat and ensure accurate cutting on larger items and thicker layers of fabric.

### PINKING SHEARS

For finishing seams or cutting curves, pinking shears are a useful tool to have in your sewing box. They can also add a decorative edge on non-woven fabrics such as felt!

# Securing your fabric

Keep a range of temporary and permanent adhesives in your tool box: a repositionable spray for appliqué, permanent glues that adhere when ironed, and a temporary glue stick for fabric, which is useful for tacking/basting zips instead of sewing by hand.

Use quality pins with large heads – this will ensure that the pins are easy to remove as you sew... and easy to spot if you drop them! For thicker fabrics or multiple layers you may need to use fabric clips, rather than pins.

# Marking your fabric

There are lots of options available to you. Air-erasable pens deliver ink that disappears after a few hours, while water-erasable ink washes away. I tend to use heat-erasable ink pens in the seam allowance – the ink will disappear using either friction or heat from the iron. Fabric pencils are useful and are available in both light and dark colours so they stand out against any fabric. Chalk is an option, but I find it can be difficult to make an accurate mark.

### SLIDING GAUGES

These tools will help to measure and mark seams and hems, and can also be used to mark curves and circles on your fabric.

# Bodkins

Safety pins are fine to help thread elastic and ribbon through channels, but it's worth investing in a bodkin to make the threading quick and simple!

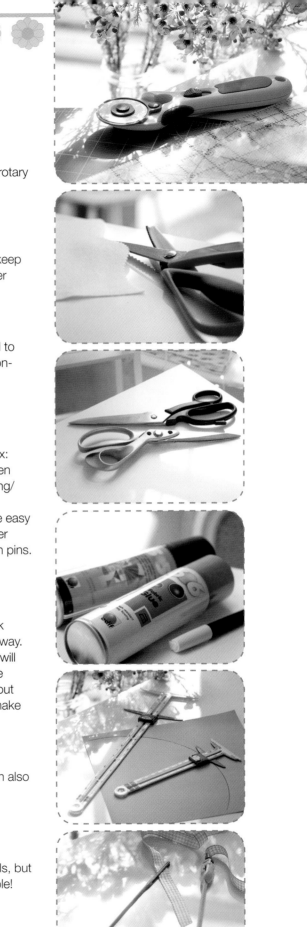

# Useful stitches

## Machine stitches

### STRAIGHT STITCH

This straight, single-line stitch (pictured below) is the most commonly used on any project. Lengthen the thread to create a tacking/basting stitch, and shorten the length of the stitch when making smaller or three-dimensional projects, as the small stitches are strong when put under the strain of stuffing.

### ZIGZAG STITCH

A decorative stitch (pictured below) that can be used to join two pieces of fabric together to create a flat seam, this stitch can also be useful to help stop raw fabric edges fraying. Shorten the length of a zigzag stitch to make a satin stitch. Perfect for appliqué, use this on the Teepee (page 40) to attach your 'grass'.

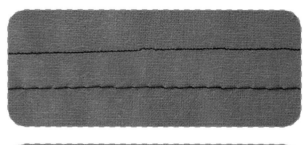

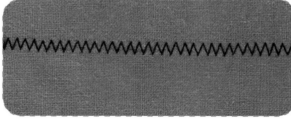

### BUTTONHOLE STITCH

Many modern machines will have a choice of buttonhole stitches. Always practise on scrap fabric first to make sure the hole is the right size and shape for your project.

## Hand stitches

### SLIP STITCH

I use this to finish off bias binding (A). Keep the stitch to a short length and try to catch just a couple of strands of the fold of the bias binding to keep the stitch as invisible as possible. (See bias binding on pages 12–13.)

### LADDER STITCH

This is the perfect stitch for closing turning gaps or making repairs in seams (B). Take the needle from one side of the opening to the opposite side, then gently pull to close the gap. Small stitches are the least visible.

### RUNNING STITCH

Tiny running stitches can be as strong as a machine straight stitch; use longer stitches for tacking/basting or gathering (C).

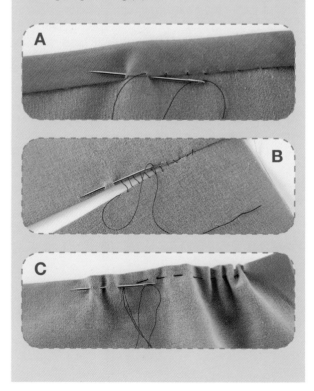

# Key techniques

## Snipping into curves

Cutting small 'V' shapes into the seam allowance of curves will help to reduce bulk and allow the seam to sit flat without puckering. Pinking shears are useful tools for speedy snipping, or a small sharp pair of scissors will do the trick!

## Cutting corners

To reduce bulk and create sharper points, cut across the seam allowances in the corners of a project that will be turned through, but be very careful not to cut through the stitches.

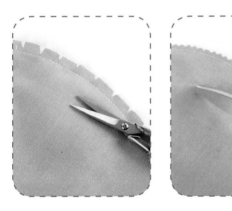

## Attaching a pompom trim

Pompom and other decorative trims really finish off a project, and can give a shop-bought look to pillow covers and tablecloths. Either sew the trim into the seam, with the pompoms facing inwards so they pop out when the item is turned, or add afterwards by topstitching by hand or on the machine.

   If you are attaching trim around a corner, put a small snip into the tape to allow the trim to turn and sit flat.

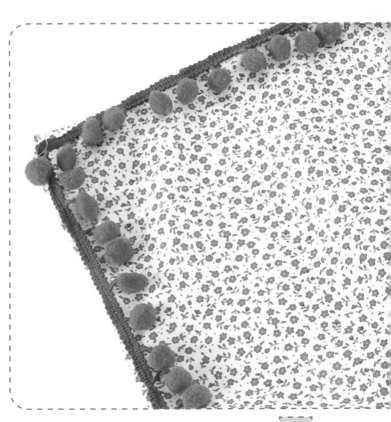

# Bias binding

I use quite a lot of bias binding in my projects as it's a simple way to finish off raw edges and it gives a professional finish. Although it can be bought in many colours and widths, I like to make my own as it's not only cost-effective, it also means I can coordinate my fabrics. Bias tape is so called because it is a strip of fabric cut at a 45-degree angle along the bias of the fabric. This allows a little 'give', so that the fabric can stretch around curves without puckering. To cut your fabric accurately you'll need a rotary cutter, rectangular ruler and cutting mat.

## MAKING BIAS BINDING

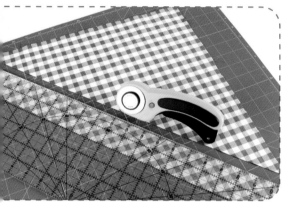  

**1** Lay your fabric squarely on the cutting mat and, using the 45-degree mark, place the ruler on the straight edge of the fabric. And cut! Use the straight side of the ruler to measure the width you need. For 2.5cm (1in) tape you'll need to cut 5cm (2in) of fabric. As you're cutting the strips, your cut line will become longer, so fold the fabric in half, matching up the diagonal edges, and cut through two, three or four layers at a time.

**2** To join the strips together, lay two pieces right sides together, overlapping at right angles. Draw a diagonal line from one corner to the other across the overlap, as shown. Pin, then sew across this line. Trim the raw edge back to around 3mm (1/8in) and press the seam open.

**3** Making bias binding involves folding over both the long edges into the centre and pressing. The easiest way to do this is to use a bias tape maker, through which you thread the tape. It folds the strip in two and you press with your iron while pulling the fabric through. If you don't have a tape maker, carefully fold both long edges to the centre of the strip and press. Be careful not to get your fingers too close to the iron!

## APPLYING BIAS BINDING

**1** To apply the binding, open up the crease lines and, right sides together, pin across the raw edge of your work. Sew with your machine along the upper crease mark.

**2** Fold the tape over the raw edge, and use slip stitch (see page 10) to sew by hand.

*Tip: continuous bias binding*

If you're applying the bias tape continuously, start by opening up the creases and folding over the end of the tape; then pin and machine sew as in step 1, below left. When you get back to the start, overlap the ends of the tape by about 5mm (¼in). Fold over and stitch as in step 2, above. Instead of slip stitching by hand you could machine topstitch.

## MITRING A CORNER

If the bias binding is attached around a curve it will stretch easily, but if you want to mitre a corner, this is how to do it.

**1** Sew along the upper crease line but stop 5mm (¼in) from the corner and back-tack to stop the stitches coming undone. Fold the tape along the second side, making a triangular pleat at the corner. Fold the pleat away from your stitch line and sew straight down the second side.

**2** Open up the tape at the corner and you should see a neat mitre forming. As you fold the tape over, mirror the same mitre on the reverse.

**3** Secure the back of the tape with slip stitch.

# Inserting a zip into a seam

Zips aren't as daunting as many people think, so don't be afraid to work with them. There are many ways to insert a zip into your project, but I find this method the easiest for pillow covers.

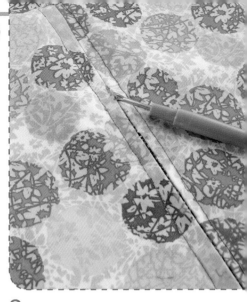

1 Allow for a 1cm (½in) seam where the zip will be inserted. Press the seam open. Place your zip facing downwards and secure with a temporary glue stick.

2 Sew a box shape around the zip, sewing from the right side to ensure a neat stitch line. Unpick the stitches over the teeth of the zip with a quick unpick.

# Piping

Piping adds a touch of class to any project, and although you can buy pre-made piping, you'll always have the right colour if you make your own.

1 For 3mm (⅛in) piping cord, cut a fabric strip on the bias, 4cm (1½in) wide. Wrap around the cord and pin the raw edges together.

2 With the zipper foot on your machine, sew alongside the cord, removing the pins as you go.

3 Pin the piping raw edges together to your fabric, and sew.

4 Sew the second section of fabric right sides together, sandwiching the piping in the middle, sewing inside the original stitch line. When you turn the fabric you'll have a lovely neat border!

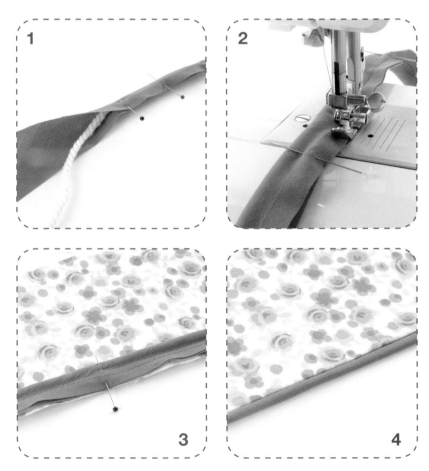

# Applying magnetic clasps

Although they are a simple way to add closures to projects, magnetic clasps don't generally come with instructions, so this may help.

1 Your clasp will be in two halves – one thin and one thick. If applying to a bag with a flap, the thicker part will go on the bag and the thinner one on the flap. Mark the position of the clasp by drawing through the backing disc.

2 Make small cuts either side of the centre spot, either with your quick unpick or a small, sharp pair of scissors. Start small – you can always make a small hole bigger, but if you make the cuts too big you'll just have holes in your fabric!

3 Push the prongs of the clasp through the slits and then the backing disc.

4 Open out the prongs on the back of the fabric. It's a good idea to place a square of fabric behind the clasp to help strengthen the closure, particularly on fine fabrics.

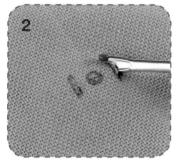
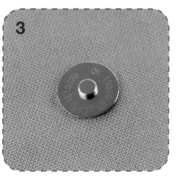

# Pompom Tablecloth

There's nothing difficult about this tablecloth; it's simply a length of fabric neatened with a trim, perfect for a quick table dressing that doesn't cost the earth!

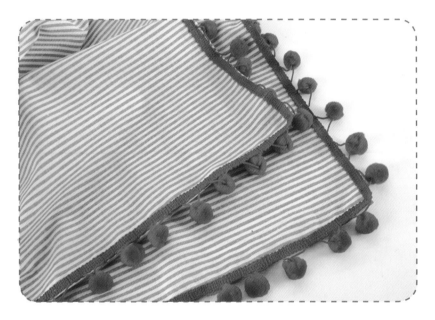

1 Turn the edges of the cloth over twice and press in place. Sew to secure the hem. Sew your pompom trim all around the hem, on the right side of the cloth, overlapping the ends to make neat. See page 11 for information on fitting the trim around corners.

## Tip

A pretty way to dress the table is to put plastic cutlery in a jar, and simply tie a ribbon around it. Drop a string of pearls into the jar and add a sprig of gypsophila for an elegant touch!

# Reverse Appliqué Heart Placemat

These pretty placemats not only decorate your table – by using heat-resistant wadding/batting they can help protect it too. Make them in any size you like, to coordinate or contrast with your tablecloth.

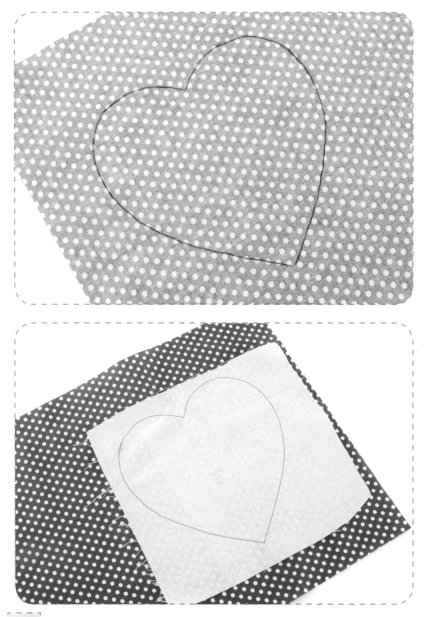

### Finished size
34.5 x 27cm (13½ x 10½in)

### What you need
71 x 28cm (28 x 11in) fabric

35.5 x 28cm (14 x 11in) thermal wadding/batting (optional)

25.5 x 51cm (10 x 20in) calico or contrasting fabric

Four strips of ribbon measuring 20.5cm (8in)

Erasable marker pen

Heart template (see page 95)

**1** Cut two pieces of fabric measuring 35.5 x 28cm (14 x 11in). Trace your heart pattern onto the wrong side of one piece, 6.5cm (2½in) in from the top and the left-hand side.

**2** Cut a 25.5cm (10in) square from the calico/contrasting fabric and pin to the right side of the fabric, over the heart shape (pin right side down, if your fabric has sides). Hold the fabric to the light to show the heart outline if you can't see it. Sew around the heart shape with a small stitch.

3 Cut out the centre of the heart, across the point and into the 'V' at the bottom of the heart.

4 Turn right side out and press.

5 Trace the heart shape onto the remaining piece of calico/contrasting fabric with an erasable marker pen. Sew three of your ribbon strips across the heart and use the fourth to make a small bow.

6 Align the cut-out heart over the ribbon-embellished heart, secure with pins or a temporary glue stick, then sew around the heart shape. Remove any pins. Sew the ribbon bow to one side of the heart.

7 Sew the two rectangles right sides together, leaving a turning gap in the bottom seam of about 7.5cm (3in). Snip across the corners. If you want to add any wadding/batting, do so now: simply pop a layer on the top and sew round as stated, leaving a turning gap.

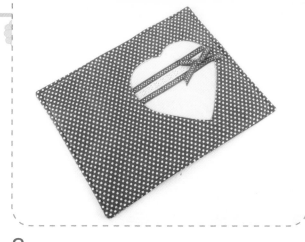

*Variation*

Here, pompom trim was added before sewing the two rectangles together, in the same way as for the Buttoned Pillow on page 36.

8 Turn right side out and press, then topstitch all around the edge.

*It's fun to make each place setting slightly different, using contrasting fabrics and trimmings.*

# Plant Pot Covers

If you want to disguise mismatched or unattractive plastic plant pots, just dress them up in these drawstring covers and you'll be proud to show them off! Use a 1.25cm (½in) seam allowance for this project.

## Finished size

My plant pots measure 23cm (9in) across and 20.5cm (8in) deep

## What you need

Per pot:
58.5 x 35.5cm
(23 x 14in) fabric
76.25cm (30in) cord or ribbon

**1** If you're using a different sized pot to mine, measure around the top of the pot, and the height.

**2** Add about 15cm (6in) to the length of your fabric, and 5cm (2in) to the width.

**3** Trim the short sides with pinking shears to prevent fraying. Fold with the short edges meeting, right sides together, and sew the seam, starting and finishing 10cm (4in) from each end. Press the seam open.

**4** Fold the top and bottom edges over by 1.25cm (½in), twice. Topstitch, creating a channel.

**5** Cut the ribbon or cord in half, then thread through each channel using a bodkin.

**6** Slip the cover over your plant pot, then gather each ribbon and tie into a bow.

# Bunting in a Bag

Bunting will brighten up indoor or outdoor living spaces for any occasion! To keep your bunting tidy when you're not using it, make a simple hanging bag (see overleaf). Use a basic or non-directional print to make the most of your fabric.

### Finished size

183 x 25.5cm (72 x 10in)

### What you need

102 x 25.5cm (40 x 10in) striped fabric
102 x 25.5cm (40 x 10in) floral fabric
Eight pompoms
3m (118in) of 2cm (¾in) wide bias binding
Strong thread
102 x 38cm (40 x 15in) contrast fabric for the bag
25.5cm (10in) of 2cm (¾in) wide bias binding

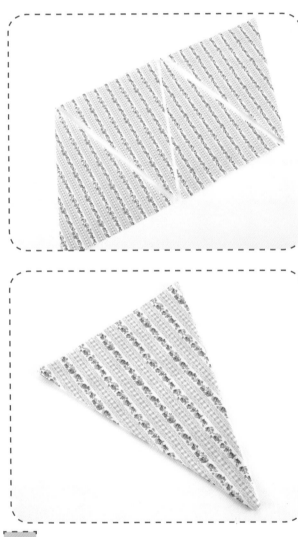

1 Cut your fabric strips into triangles measuring 20.5cm (8in) across the top and 25.5cm (10in) deep. The easiest way to do this is to use a rotary cutter, ruler and mat and to cut a 'zigzag' across the strips of fabric. You need to cut eight triangles from each fabric.

2 Sew each pair of pennants (triangles) right sides together, leaving the top edge open. Snip across the point, turn right side out and press.

3 When all eight pennants are sewn, trim straight across the tops. Hand sew a pompom to the point of each triangle with strong thread.

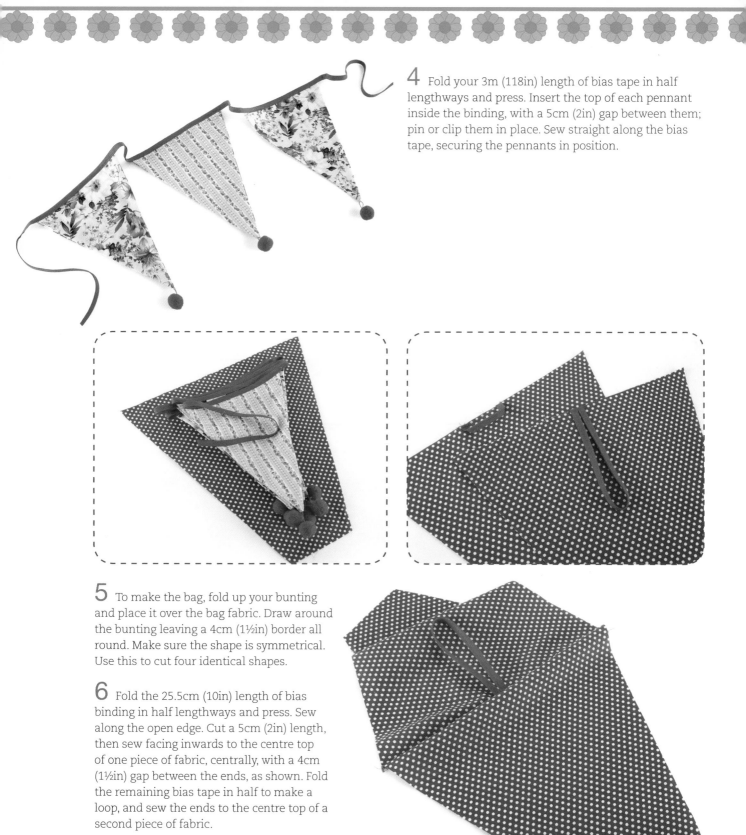

**4** Fold your 3m (118in) length of bias tape in half lengthways and press. Insert the top of each pennant inside the binding, with a 5cm (2in) gap between them; pin or clip them in place. Sew straight along the bias tape, securing the pennants in position.

**5** To make the bag, fold up your bunting and place it over the bag fabric. Draw around the bunting leaving a 4cm (1½in) border all round. Make sure the shape is symmetrical. Use this to cut four identical shapes.

**6** Fold the 25.5cm (10in) length of bias binding in half lengthways and press. Sew along the open edge. Cut a 5cm (2in) length, then sew facing inwards to the centre top of one piece of fabric, centrally, with a 4cm (1½in) gap between the ends, as shown. Fold the remaining bias tape in half to make a loop, and sew the ends to the centre top of a second piece of fabric.

**7** Sew a remaining fabric piece right sides together to the top of each piece with a loop.

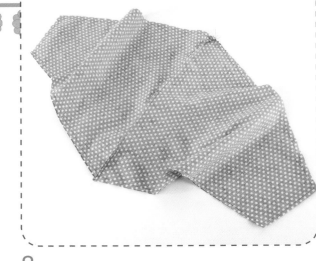

**8** Place the two panels right sides together, matching the seams. Sew all the way around, leaving a turning gap of about 7.5cm (3in) in one side.

**9** Turn right side out and sew the turning gap closed. Push the lining inside the bag and press, then topstitch around the top.

**10** Pop your bunting inside!

# Frilled Chair Pillow

What a stylish way to add a touch of colour and comfort to your garden chairs! As you're making your own pattern, these pretty pillows can be made to fit any size of seat. If yours is much larger than mine, be sure to make extra frill.

1 To make the pattern, push the paper into the shape of the seat of the chair and crease around the edge.

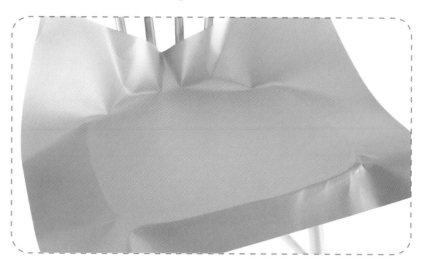

2 Cut out the seat shape. Fold the paper pattern in half to make sure it is symmetrical.

## Finished size
43.5 x 40.5cm (17 x 16in)

## What you need
114.5 x 76.25cm (45 x 30in) fabric (adjust this measurement if your seat is much larger or smaller than mine)

1.5m (60in) of 1cm (½in) wide ribbon

Approximately 250g (9oz) toy filler

Fork

Paper to make a template

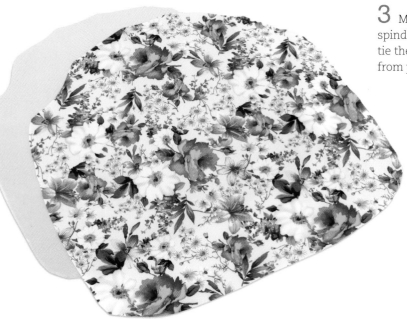

**3** Mark on your pattern the position of the spindles on the back of the chair you'd like to tie the seat pad to. Cut out two fabric pieces from your pattern.

**4** Cut a length of fabric measuring 10 x 343cm (4 x 135in) – you'll need to join a few pieces. Fold the strip in half wrong sides together and press.

**5** Secure the raw edge of one end of the fabric strip with the needle, 2.5cm (1in) from the end. Thread your fabric through one of the tines of your fork.

**6** Turn the fork over to make a pleat, remove the fork, then sew. Repeat all along the fabric strip, leaving 2.5cm (1in) unsewn at the end.

**7** Fold the ends of the pleated strip over by 1cm (½in) and press. Your frill should be long enough to go around three sides of your pillow.

**8** Sew the frill, facing inwards and right sides together, to one of the fabric seat pieces. As you approach the corners, add a few extra small pleats so that the frill sits flat when turned. Trim off any excess.

**9** Cut the ribbon in half and fold each piece in half again. Sew the folded pieces, facing inwards, to the spindle positions you marked on the pattern. Take the two sides of the cover and sew right sides together, leaving a turning gap in the back edge of about 13cm (5in). Turn right side out. Fill lightly with toy filler and hand sew the opening closed.

**10** Place on your chair seat and tie the ribbons around the spindles on the back of the chair.

# Patchwork Picnic Mat

This picnic mat has a laminated backing to help keep it dry, and it would also make a useful playmat for the kids. To enlarge the size, simply add more squares and make the backing bigger. Use a 5mm (¼in) seam allowance.

**1** Cut thirteen checked and twelve spotted squares, each measuring 20.5 x 20.5cm (8 x 8in). Sew alternating squares right sides together in a row of five, starting and ending with spotted fabric.

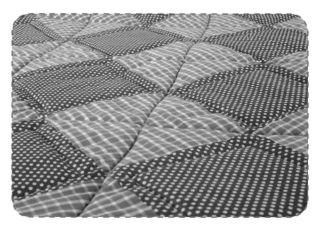

**2** Sew the next five pieces together starting and ending with a checked fabric square, and continue until all your squares are used. Sew the strips right sides together, matching the seams.

**3** Spray the wrong side of the fabric with adhesive and place on top of the wadding/batting. Draw diagonal lines across the checked pieces with your erasable marker, then sew. Sew around each spotted square, 2.5cm (1in) in from the seam; finally sew 3.25cm (1¼in) in from the raw edges of the patchwork.

4 Trim the edges of the mat to make it square. Place on top of the oilcloth and secure with adhesive; smooth it to make sure there are no wrinkles, then trim the oilcloth to the size of the mat. Sew around the edge.

5 Apply bias binding around the edge of the mat (see pages 12–13), mitring the corners and overlapping the ends to make neat.

6 To make the carry strap, cut one strip of checked and one strip of spotted fabric, each measuring 66 x 15.25cm (26 x 6in). Fuse fleece to the wrong side of one piece. Use your circle template to trim one end of each section.

7 Use adhesive to secure the two pieces together, wrong sides facing. Apply bias binding all around the edge, mitring the square corners.

8 Cut a strip of checked fabric measuring 10 x 20.5cm (4 x 8in) for the handle, fold in half lengthways and press, unfold, then fold the edges to the centre, fold in half again and press.

**9** Take the two long edges and fold back on themselves – sew across each short end.

**10** Turn back again so that the short seams are in the inside, then topstitch all the way around. Sew each end of the handle to the curved end of the strap, in a box shape, 15.25cm (6in) from the end. The handle should be raised.

**11** Sew one half of the hook-and-loop fastening to the square end of the strap on the top side, 5cm (2in) from the end, and the remaining half of the fastening to the opposite side of the curved end, 4cm (1½in) from the curve.

**12** Fold your mat neatly into thirds, then fold each end to the centre and in half again, secure the carry strap around the mat and you're ready to go!

*To make the bees and ladybirds/ ladybugs shown here, see page 66.*

# Buttoned Pillow

Even the plainest chair can be well dressed and comfy with a stylish pillow! I like mine plump; if you prefer a flatter pillow, cut your fabric 1cm (½in) larger all around.

## Finished size

29.5 x 29.5cm (11½ x 11½in), not including trim

## What you need

76.25 x 30.5cm (30 x 12in) patterned fabric

30.5 x 7.5cm (12 x 3in) strip of lightweight fusible interfacing

45.75 x 30.5cm (18 x 12in) plain fabric

Three buttons

115cm (45in) pompom trim

30.5cm (12in) square pillow pad

1 Cut one square of patterned fabric measuring 30.5 x 30.5cm (12 x 12in), another patterned piece measuring 30.5 x 45.75cm (12 x 18in) and one plain piece measuring 45.75 x 30.5cm (18 x 12in).

2 Fold the long patterned piece in half, wrong sides together and press. Open out, then place the interfacing strip along the crease on the wrong side of the fabric and iron to fuse.

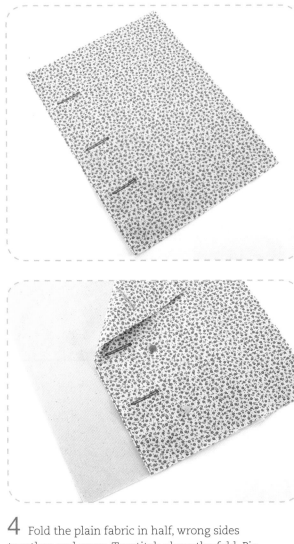

3 Fold back in half again, then topstitch along the fold. Measure and mark halfway and 2.5cm (1in) from the folded edge to position the centre buttonhole, then 9cm (3½in) either side of this mark for the remaining two buttonholes. Sew the buttonholes on your machine.

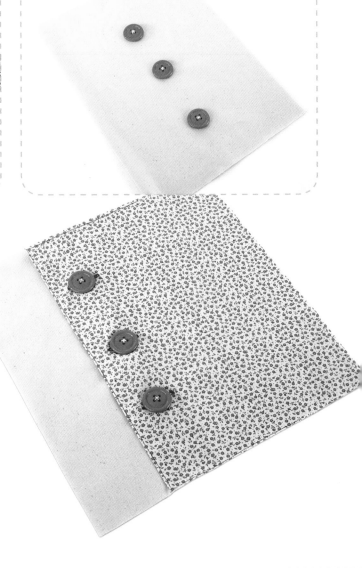

4 Fold the plain fabric in half, wrong sides together and press. Topstitch along the fold. Pin the patterned piece, overlapping the plain, to make a 30.5cm (12in) square – the topstitched edges should sit in the centre. Mark the plain fabric through the centre of the buttonholes to mark the position of the buttons.

5 Sew the buttons to the plain fabric.

6 Overlap the plain and patterned pieces once more and fasten the buttons. Tack/baste the two pieces together along the overlapping top and bottom edges.

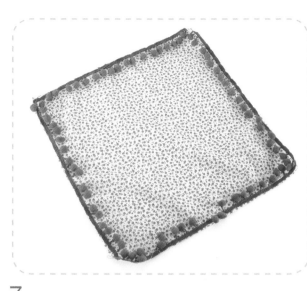

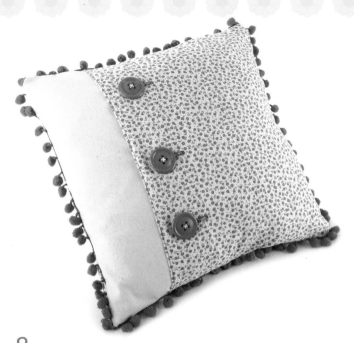

**7** Sew the pompom trim, facing inwards, around the remaining square of patterned fabric, overlapping the ends to make neat.

**8** Sew the two pillow pieces right sides together, ensuring that you do not sew over the pompoms. Snip across the corners, turn right side out and press. Insert your pillow pad.

## *Variation*

If buttonholes and trimmings are a bit daunting for you, sew up to step 3, leave off the buttonholes and attach three 20.5cm (8in) lengths of ribbon instead over the marks. Place this section over the folded plain piece (as in step 4), mark the plain fabric adjacent to the ribbons, then sew on three more ribbons over the marks. Tack/baste along the raw edges to join the two pieces together (as in step 6). Remove the pins, sew the two pillow cover pieces right sides together, snip off the corners, turn right side out, insert your pillow pad and finally tie the ribbons into bows.

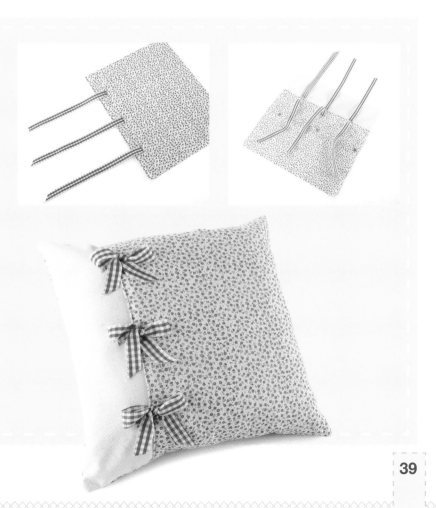

# Teepee

The kids will love playing in their very own teepee in the garden! The ends of the poles can be pushed into soft ground; if the teepee comes inside I'd suggest it's kept on carpet to stop it slipping.

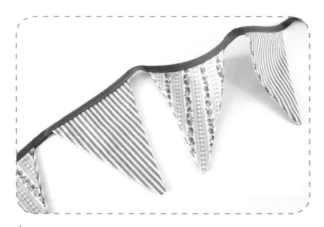

**1** Make up fourteen bunting pennants measuring 15.25cm (6in) deep and 12.75cm (5in) across the top (see bunting on pages 24–27). Sew the pennants to the bias binding, with a 2.5cm (1in) gap between them.

**2** Cut out four large teepee pieces (diagram A), two mirror-image front panels (diagram B) and one top front piece (diagram C). Cut your green fabric into 41cm (16in) strips, then make zigzag cuts across the fabric to make grass – you'll be able to cut two grass strips from each piece if you make the zigzag cut across the centre of the fabric.

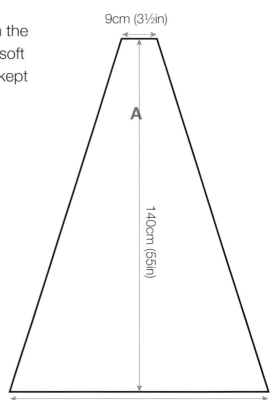

9cm (3½in)

**A**

140cm (55in)

91.5cm (36in)

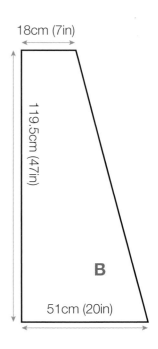

18cm (7in)

119.5cm (47in)

**B**

51cm (20in)

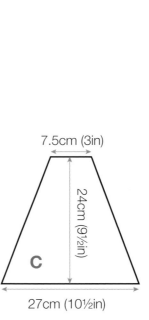

7.5cm (3in)

24cm (9½in)

**C**

27cm (10½in)

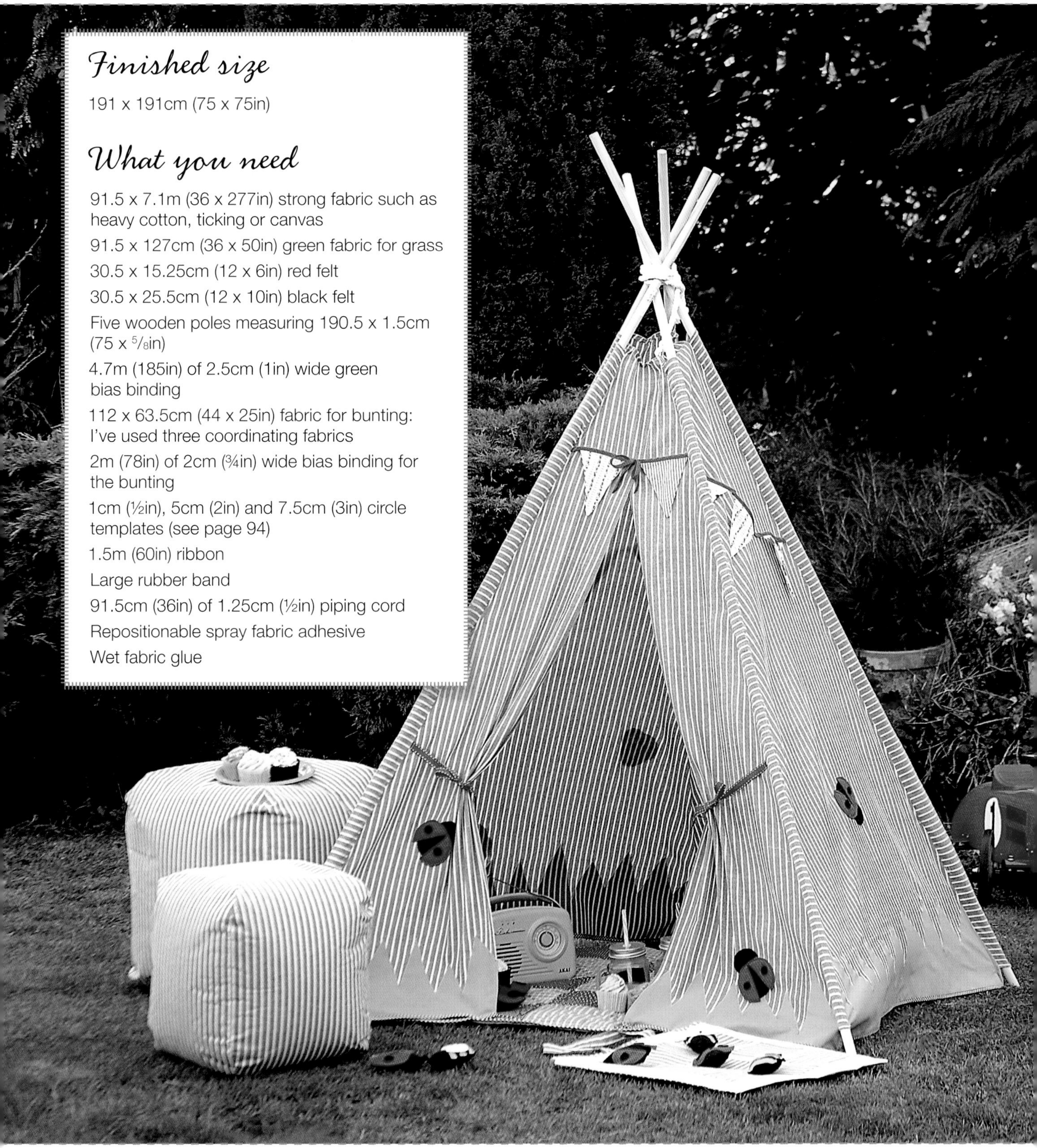

## Finished size

191 x 191cm (75 x 75in)

## What you need

91.5 x 7.1m (36 x 277in) strong fabric such as heavy cotton, ticking or canvas

91.5 x 127cm (36 x 50in) green fabric for grass

30.5 x 15.25cm (12 x 6in) red felt

30.5 x 25.5cm (12 x 10in) black felt

Five wooden poles measuring 190.5 x 1.5cm (75 x $^5/_8$in)

4.7m (185in) of 2.5cm (1in) wide green bias binding

112 x 63.5cm (44 x 25in) fabric for bunting: I've used three coordinating fabrics

2m (78in) of 2cm (¾in) wide bias binding for the bunting

1cm (½in), 5cm (2in) and 7.5cm (3in) circle templates (see page 94)

1.5m (60in) ribbon

Large rubber band

91.5cm (36in) of 1.25cm (½in) piping cord

Repositionable spray fabric adhesive

Wet fabric glue

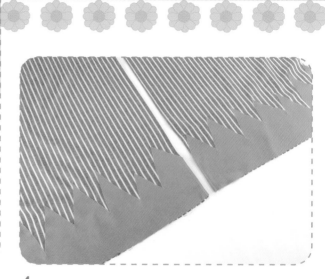

**3** Spray the wrong sides of the grass strips with adhesive and place across the bottom of each teepee piece. Satin stitch around the zigzag edge.

**4** Take the two front panels, and fold the long straight sides to the wrong side by 1cm (½in) twice and topstitch to hem.

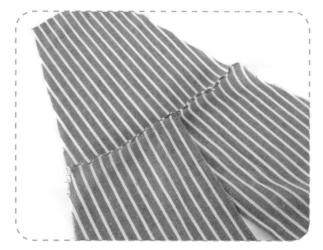

**5** Sew the two front panels wrong sides together to the front top piece, matching outside edges and overlapping in the centre. Trim the seam to 5mm (¼in).

**6** Press the seam upwards, then sew two of the pennants, with binding, across the front of the seam. This method will hide the raw edge of the fabric and keep the seam neat on the inside of the teepee. Make a bow from leftover bias binding and add to the centre of the opening.

**7** To make the ladybirds/ladybugs: cut eight 7.5cm (3in) red felt circles, eight 7.5cm (3in) black felt circles, eight 5cm (2in) black felt circles and sixteen 1cm (½in) black felt circles (see templates on page 94). Cut into each red circle straight across the centre, but not all the way through. Glue the small circles to each side of the red 'wings', glue the small black 'head' circles over the larger black 'bodies' with wet glue, then glue the wings on top.

8 Position the ladybirds/ladybugs around the teepee wherever you like, then sew around the wings to secure.

9 Lay out the five teepee panels, and arrange the bunting across each section, cutting the strip in between every third pennant. Tack/baste the ends of the bunting to the edges of the fabric.

10 Cut your ribbon into four equal lengths. Measure halfway along each outer side of the front panels, and tack/baste one piece of ribbon to either side of the fabric.

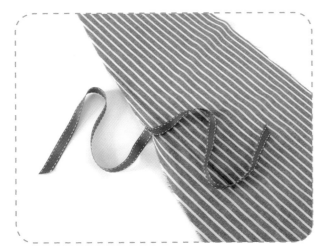

11 Cut five strips of teepee fabric measuring 10 x 140cm (4 x 55in). Fold over each short end twice and sew to hem, then fold each strip in half lengthways, wrong sides together, and press.

**12** Sew each strip, facing inwards, to one long side of each teepee piece, leaving an equal gap at the top and bottom of the fabric. These strips will form the channels for your poles.

**13** Sew the teepee panels together, right sides facing, sandwiching the channels in between the sections.

**14** Trim the seams to 3mm (⅛in). Fold each section so that the channel sits on the edge of the seam, and sew a line 5mm (¼in) from the seam – this will trap the raw edges on the inside and make them neat. This is a little like a French seam.

**15** Fold your bias tape in half lengthways and press. Fold this around the bottom of the teepee, turning the short ends in to make neat. Sew all the way around.

**16** Turn the top of the teepee over twice by 1cm (½in) and sew to hem.

**17** Push the poles through the channels. Take your rubber band and wrap around the crossing poles at the top of the teepee, before tying with piping cord. The rubber band will help to stop the poles from slipping.

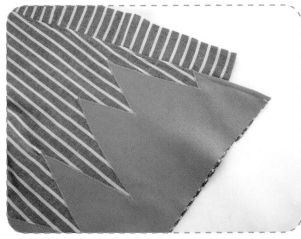

*Tip*
If you find that the fabric moves down the poles, punch a staple to the top and bottom of each channel to secure it.

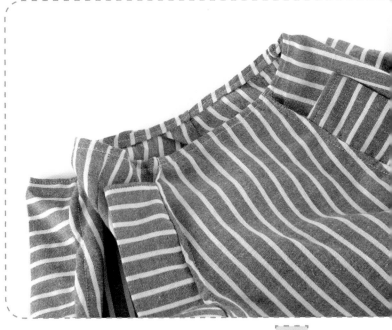

# Knotted Bolster Pillow

This has to be the easiest and quickest way to cover a bolster pillow of any size! My pillow pad measures 30.5cm (12in) in length and 33cm (13in) in circumference. Use a 5mm (¼in) seam allowance.

*Finished size*

56 x 11.5cm (22 x 4½in), including the ties

*What you need*

91.5 x 35.5cm (36 x 14in) fabric
Bolster pillow pad

1 Measure the length and circumference of your pillow. Cut your fabric three times the length and 2.5cm (1in) wider than the pad. Mine therefore measures 91.5 x 35.5cm (36 x 14in). Fold the short ends over twice and topstitch to hem. Fold the fabric in half lengthways, right sides together, and sew to make a tube.

2 Turn right side out. Push your bolster pad inside leaving the same amount of fabric free at each end.

3 Knot the fabric close to the pad at each end.

47

# Heart Decorations

Fill these pretty decorations with dried lavender or drizzle the filling with citronella essential oil to create a fragrant display on your table. The potted versions would make fun place names if you embroidered them with the names of your guests!

## Finished size

12.75 x 12.75cm (5 x 5in)

## What you need

Two 25.5cm (10in) squares of fabric

Toy filler

30.5cm (12in) wooden craft stick

Small plant pot

Spray paint (for the pot)

Florists' oasis

30.5cm (12in) ribbon

Handful of small buttons

Strong wet glue

Heart template (see page 95)

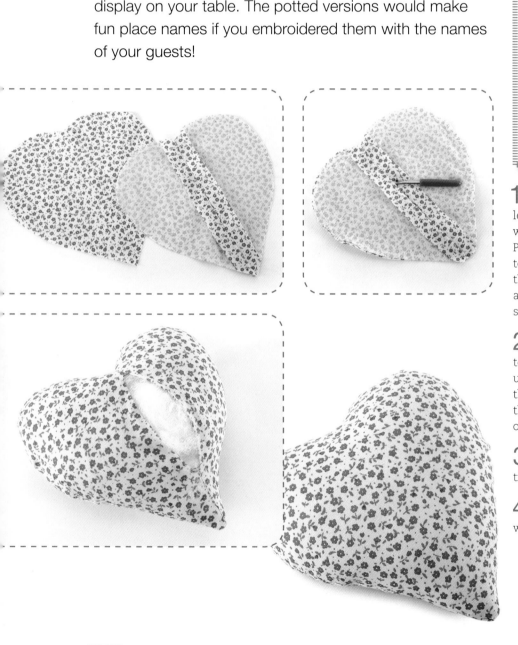

**1** Cut one square in half lengthways, then sew back together with a 1cm (½in) seam allowance. Press the seam open, place your template over the seam and trace, then cut out the heart shape. Cut another heart from the remaining square of fabric.

**2** Sew the two hearts right sides together. Take a quick-unpick and undo approximately 5cm (2in) from the centre of the seam. Snip across the point and into the 'V' at the top of the heart.

**3** Turn right side out and stuff tightly with toy filler.

**4** Hand-sew the opening closed with a ladder stitch.

**5** Undo a couple of stitches at the point of the heart. Dab a little wet glue on the end of your craft stick and push it into the stitching gap. Make sure the stick goes into the filler far enough to stop the heart from wobbling. Tie a bow around the join with the ribbon. Sew through the holes in one of the buttons, then glue to the stick, just underneath the bow.

**6** Spray paint your plant pot. Push the oasis inside the pot; glue in place if you wish.

**7** Push the heart into the oasis. Drizzle wet glue over the top of the oasis and sprinkle the buttons over the top.

# Bean Bag Stool

Need extra seating? Why not make your own stylish and comfortable cubes? Buy polystyrene beans by the cubic foot and make sure you buy the ones in netting, as loose beans are static and will stick to everything! Use a 1cm (½in) seam allowance.

## Finished size

30.5 x 30.5 x 30.5cm (12 x 12 x 12in)

## What you need

132 x 66cm (52 x 26in) strong fabric, such as canvas, ticking or denim

132 x 66cm (52 x 26in) fusible interfacing, medium weight

30.5cm (12in) zip

Pattern paper, pen and ruler

1 cubic foot of bean bag beans

Fabric glue pen

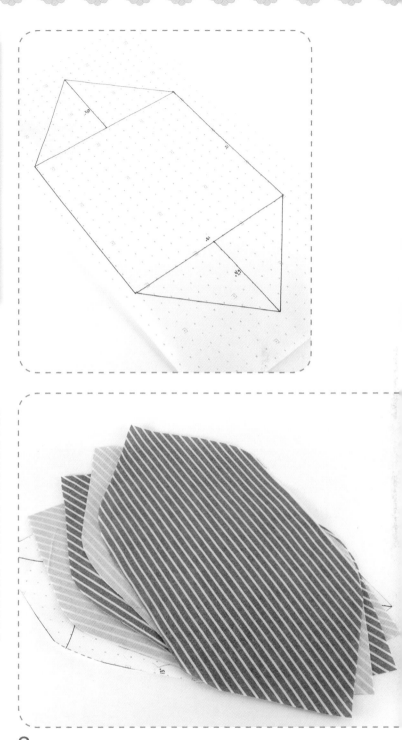

**1** Draw a 33cm (13in) square on your pattern paper. Take a 16.5cm (6½in) line from the centre of two opposite sides, and join to make a triangle on each end.

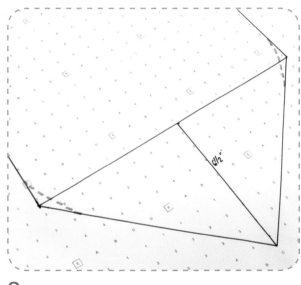

**2** Draw a curve at each corner.

**3** Cut out your pattern, then fold it in half to make sure the shape is symmetrical; adjust if necessary. Fuse the interfacing to the wrong side of your fabric and cut out four pieces using your pattern.

4 Take two pieces and sew right sides together along the straight edge. Press the seam open. Place the zip face down over the top, secure with a fabric glue pen, and sew the zip in place with a rectangle of stitches.

5 Use a quick unpick to open the stitches over the zip.

6 Sew the edges at the top and bottom of the zip together, up to the points of the triangles, right sides facing. Take the remaining two pieces, and sew right sides together along one edge, again, from point to point. With the zip open, sew the two sections of the stool together, right sides facing.

### Tip
Remember to leave the zip partly open when you stitch the side seams so that you can turn the cover the right way out afterwards.

7 Turn right side out. Stuff your beans inside the stool; take your time with this, as they are quite fluid!

**8** Close the zip and you're finished!

# Piped Box Pillow

This useful technique creates firm, box-shaped chair pillows and would work equally well for floor pillows or bench seats. The piping can be left off if you're not too confident, but it does add a professional finishing touch and makes the pillow a little more sturdy.

## Finished size

44.5 x 44.5 x 5cm
(17½ x 17½ x 2in)

## What you need

89 x 44.5cm (35 x 17½in)
striped fabric

180.75 x 5cm (71 x 2in)
spotted fabric

183 x 8cm (72 x 3in)
striped fabric for the piping

3.7m (144in) of 5mm (¼in)
piping cord

46cm (18in) zip

43.25cm (17in) square
foam pad, 5cm (2in) deep

**1** Cut your foam to the size of the chair seat: mine is 43.25cm (17in) square and has slightly rounded corners. A sharp knife will be easier to cut with than scissors.

**2** Cut your piping fabric into two strips measuring 4 x 183cm (1½ x 72in) – you may have to join a few pieces together. If this is the case, join the strips at a 45-degree angle to make the seam less visible (as for bias binding, page 12).

**3** Cut the piping cord in half. Wrap the fabric around each length of cord and sew close to the cord with the zipper foot on your machine.

**4** Cut two pieces of striped fabric measuring 44.5cm (17½in) square, and slightly round the corners to match the shape of the foam pad. Sew the piping, facing inwards, around one piece of fabric; overlap the ends of the cord so they are facing away from the fabric (as shown), and snip into the seam allowance as you approach the corners. Repeat with the remaining piece.

**5** Cut one length of spotted fabric measuring 135 x 5cm (53 x 2in), and one measuring 45.75 x 5cm (18 x 2in). Take the smaller length, cut in half lengthways, and sew the zip in between the two pieces.

**6** Trim back if necessary to make the zip panel 5cm (2in) wide. Sew right sides together to the ends of the longer strip to make a loop.

**7** Pin the loop around one of the seat pieces, right sides together, with the zip sitting across the back of the pillow. Sew, removing the pins as you go.

**8** With the zip open, sew the second side of the seat in place in the same way. Turn right side out and insert your foam pad.

*The finished pillow*

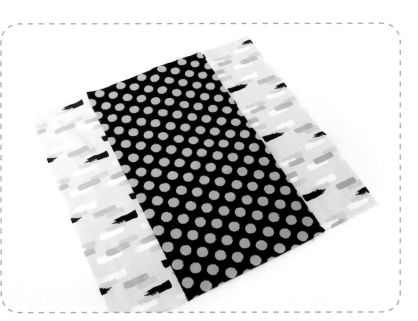

# Bolster Pillow

This classy bolster cover is a lot easier to make than it looks, and adds an elegant touch to outdoor furniture. Pair it with the pillow on page 54 for an opulent look.

**1** Spray the wrong side of your contrast fabric, and place centrally on top of the base fabric.

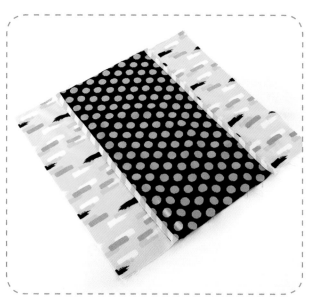

2 Fold your bias binding in half lengthways and press. I've used the binding in this way to create a thick border, which will add a little dimension to the cover. Cut in half.

3 Pin, then sew a strip of binding along each edge of the contrast fabric strip, covering the raw edges. Remove the pins. Trim off the excess binding.

4 Fold the cover in half, right sides together, and sew, leaving 2.5cm (1in) unsewn at each end.

**5** Press the 'unsewn seam' open at each end. Fold over each end of the bolster by 1cm (½in) then 1cm (½in) again; sew to form channels for the ribbon.

**6** Turn right side out. Cut your ribbon in half, pop a safety pin or bodkin on one end and thread through one channel.

**7** Pull the ribbon to gather the fabric, then tie it in a bow. Push your pillow pad inside the cover, thread the remaining ribbon through the second channel, gather and tie in a bow.

**8** Your bolster pillow cover is complete!

*Tip*
Don't choose fabric that is too thick, or you'll find the end of the pillow doesn't close fully when gathered.

# Mitred Tablecloth

Turn any garden table into the best dressed piece of furniture with a classic mitred tablecloth, I've chosen an elegant metallic fabric but this project would work equally well using a pretty floral or a fun spot print.

## Finished size

137 x 137cm (54 x 54in); made to fit my circular table which is 89cm (35in) across

## What you need

114.5 x 114.5cm (45 x 45in) spotted fabric

165 x 102cm (65 x 40in) striped fabric

Ruler and marking pen

Pinking shears

1 Cut the striped fabric into four 165 x 25.5cm (65 x 10in) strips. Note that you will be joining these, so the top stripe should be the same colour and depth on each one. Sew the strips to each side of the spotted square, centrally, leaving an overhang of 25.5cm (10in) on each side.

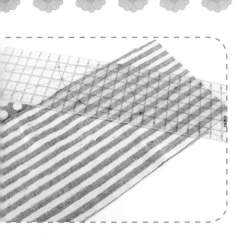

**2** Fold the long sides of the strips right sides together, lay flat and pin. The spotted fabric should be folded in half at a 45-degree angle. Take a ruler and marking pen, and draw a line from the folded edge of the spotted fabric, across the striped border at 45 degrees.

**3** Sew along this line and trim away the excess striped fabric with pinking shears to neaten the seam.

**4** Repeat with all four corners. Open out the seams and press. Cut 5mm (¼in) from the point across each corner.

**5** Fold the corners over by 5mm (¼in) and press.

**6** Turn the whole hem over by 5mm (¼in) twice and sew. By snipping across the corners, a neat mitre will form.

**7** One final press and you're ready to set the table!

# Rustic Table Accessories

Give a rustic, handmade look to your table with these simple accessories. Complete the look with vintage crates and a few pillows on the floor for comfortable seating.

## *Finished size*

43.5 x 152.5cm (17 x 60in)

## *What you need*

43 x 152.5cm (17 x 60in) burlap/hessian: 152.5cm (60in) was the width of my burlap/hessian, so I've left the fringed selvedge on

5.1m (200in) of 1cm (½in) wide ribbon

White fabric paint

Sponge dauber

Bodkin

Heart templates (see page 95)

## *Tip*

A tip for cutting burlap/hessian straight: pull one of the stringy threads out of the fabric and cut along the gap it leaves – guaranteed straight lines every time!

## Table Runner

1 Cut your burlap/hessian to size. Sew a zigzag stitch all around the edge to prevent fraying, or allow to fray deliberately. Measure 5cm (2in) from each side, and pull approximately six threads out to make a gap of 1cm (½in) along each edge. Save the string threads – you'll find them useful for decorating your candle jars (see page 65)!

2 Cut out your heart templates as stencils and, using your fabric paint and a dauber, paint hearts randomly over the ends of the runner. Make sure you cover your work surface as the paint will seep through the burlap/hessian. Leave to dry.

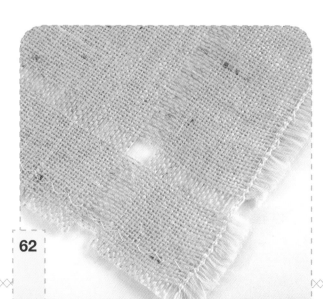

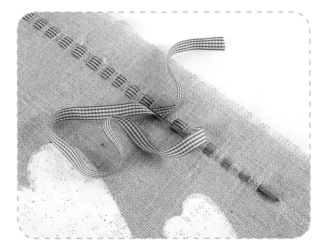

3 Weave ribbon through the gaps in the burlap/hessian, leaving 15.25cm (6in) overhanging at each corner to tie in a bow. A bodkin will help thread the ribbon. The ribbon will try to twist, so persevere!

4 Tie the ribbon at the corners into bows.

## Finished size

1.5m (59in) long

## What you need

100 x 27cm (39 x 10½in) burlap/hessian

1.5m (59in) bias binding

White fabric paint

Sponge dauber

Heart templates (see page 95)

# Bunting

The raw edges on this bunting give it a rustic feel, and make it so easy and quick to make! If this is for a special occasion, try painting words or initials on the fabric instead of hearts. Cut your bunting pennants into triangles measuring 20.5cm (8in) across the top and 25.5cm (10in) deep. Paint as you wish, then fold and sew a strip of bias binding across the top. Simple!

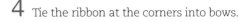

# Candle Jar with Ribbon

## Finished size

My jam jar is 10cm (4in) tall

## What you need

Jam jar

A small amount of burlap/hessian

A small amount of ribbon

Silk flowers and glue (optional)

**1** Cut a length of burlap/hessian to the height of your jar, and long enough to wrap around and slightly overlap. Fray a few rows of thread on each side, then pull away approximately six rows of threads 1cm (½in) from the top. Weave ribbon through the gaps, starting and stopping in the centre of the burlap/hessian.

**2** Wrap around your jar and pull the ribbon tight. Tie the ends in a bow and trim if necessary. Glue a couple of silk flowers over the bow to decorate.

# Stencilled Candle Jar

## Finished size

My jam jar is 10cm (4in) tall

## What you need

Jam jar

A small amount of burlap/hessian

White fabric paint

Sponge dauber

Heart templates (see page 95)

Cut your burlap/hessian long enough to wrap around your jar, and stencil a row of hearts in the same way as for your table runner. Wrap around your jar when the paint is dry, and simply tie some spare string threads around the jar to secure.

# Tic Tac Toe

Using colourful garden insects, this fun game is entertainment for the whole family, at home or on the go! The bag serves as a game board as well as handy storage.

## Finished size

43.25 x 44cm (17 x 17¼in), not including handles

## What you need

91.5 x 101.5cm (36 x 40in) striped fabric
30.5 x 46cm (12 x 18in) white fabric
86.5 x 43.25cm (34 x 17in) medium fusible interfacing
41 x 51cm (16 x 20in) black felt
15.25 x 23cm (6 x 9in) red felt
46 x 7.5cm (18 x 3in) yellow felt
18 x 7.5cm (7 x 3in) white felt
Toy filler
2.5cm (1in), 5cm (2in) and 7.5cm (3in) circle templates (see page 94)
Insect wing template (see page 95)
Pen and paper to make a template
Strong wet fabric glue
Magnetic snap fastener

1 Draw around your 7.5cm (3in) circle template, then overlap the 5cm (2in) circle by half to make the shape of the ladybird/ladybug and bee bodies.

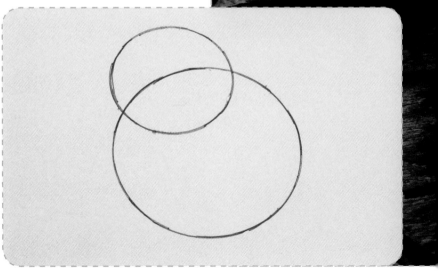

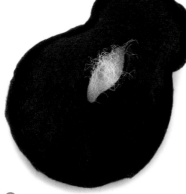

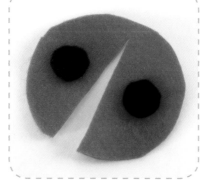

**2** Cut out the template, and use this to cut out twenty-four black felt pieces. To make the ladybirds/ladybugs, sew together 12 pieces in pairs, Make a small cut in one side of each body and stuff lightly with toy filler. Hand sew the opening closed.

**3** Cut six 7.5cm (3in) circles from red felt, and twelve 2.5cm (1in) circles from black felt. Cut through the centre of each red circle but not quite all the way across, then glue a black circle to each half.

**4** Glue the wings to the back of the ladybird/ladybug body.

**5** To make the bees, cut the yellow felt into 1cm (½in) strips. Glue three strips across six black felt bodies.

**6** Sew the remaining six body shapes to the striped pieces.

**7** Cut a small hole in each body, and stuff lightly with toy filler.

**8** Hand sew the opening closed. Cut twelve wing shapes from white felt using the template; glue two wings to the neck of each bee.

**9** You now have six bees and six ladybirds/ladybugs.

**10** To make the tote, cut nine 12.75cm (5in) squares from striped fabric.

**11** Cut two strips of white fabric measuring 42 x 2.5cm (16½ x 1in), and six strips measuring 12.75 x 2.5cm (5 x 1in). Sew the squares right sides together in strips of three, with a 12.75cm (5in) white strip in between each square.

**12** Sew these strips together in turn, divided by a 42cm (16½in) strip of white fabric.

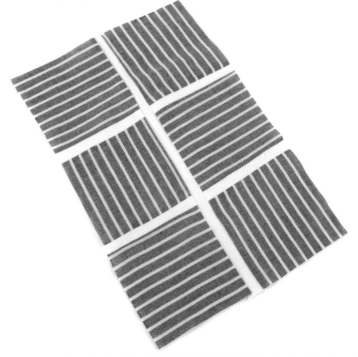

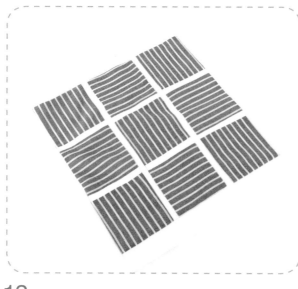

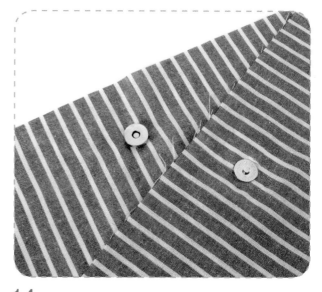

**13** When you have all nine squares sewn, trim any excess white fabric back to make a neat square. Cut four white strips of fabric measuring 45.75 x 5cm (18 x 2in). Sew to each side of the square block to make a border. Trim the whole shape to 44.5cm (17½in) square.

**14** For the lining, cut two pieces of striped fabric measuring 44.5 x 45.75cm (17½ x 18in). Fix one half of the magnetic snap fastener to either side of the top of the lining, centrally, 4cm (1½in) from the top. Fuse interfacing to the wrong sides of both outer pieces.

**15** To make the handles, cut two strips of striped fabric measuring 10 x 45.75cm (4 x 18in). Fold in half lengthways and press, then fold the long edges to the centre, fold in half again and press.

**16** Topstitch along each edge.

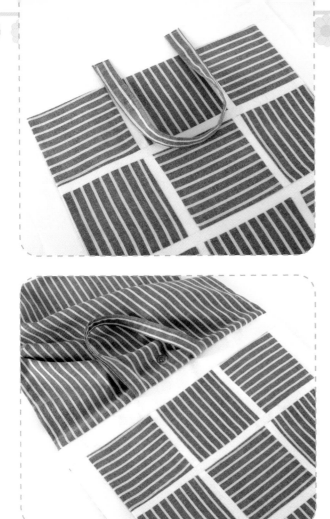

**17** Cut a 43.5cm (17in) square of stripe fabric for the back of the bag. Tack/baste the handles to both the front and back sides of the bag, facing downwards, 16.5cm (6½in) from either side.

**18** Sew the tops of the outer pieces right sides together to the tops of the lining pieces, sandwiching the handles in the middle.

**19** Sew these two sections right sides together, matching the seams. Leave a turning gap of about 12.75cm (5in) in the bottom of the lining. Snip across the corners, turn right side out and sew the opening closed.

**20** Push the lining inside the bag. As the lining is slightly longer, a border will form around the top. Topstitch all round the top of the bag.

**21** Take turns placing your bees and ladybirds/ladybugs on the squares... the first to make three in a row wins!

# Round Pillow

Making your own chair pads adds style and comfort to chairs of any size. If you're painting your chairs, try coordinating the colour with your fabric!

## Finished size

My seat pad measures 46cm (18in) across

## What you need

51 x 102cm (20 x 40in) floral fabric

41cm (16in) zip

46cm (18in) round pillow pad

Circle template or sliding gauge: measure across your chair seat, then add 5cm (2in). My seat measures 43.25cm (17in) across: I cut my circle 48.25cm (19in) across

Fabric glue stick

Pinking shears

1 Cut your fabric into two squares. Cut one square in half, then sew right sides together again with a 1cm (½in) seam allowance. Press the seam open.

2 Place your zip face down over the seam and secure with a fabric glue stick. Sew all around the zip, creating a rectangle of stitches.

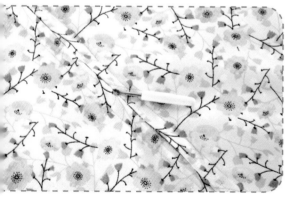

3 Unpick the stitches over the zip with a quick unpick.

4 Use your circle template or sliding gauge to make two circles, one on each piece of fabric. With the zip open, sew the two circles right sides together. Trim the seams with pinking shears.

5 Turn right side out and insert your pillow pad.

# BBQ Tool Roll

Keep your tools tidy and organized with this handy roll. Pad it well to help protect against sharp points and edges, and use a 1cm (½in) seam allowance.

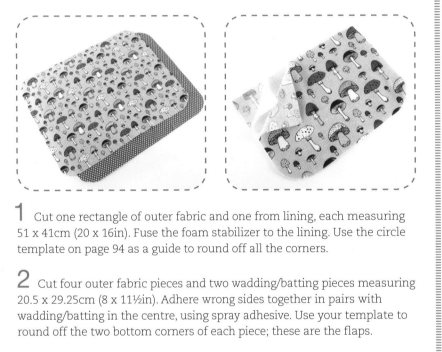

**1** Cut one rectangle of outer fabric and one from lining, each measuring 51 x 41cm (20 x 16in). Fuse the foam stabilizer to the lining. Use the circle template on page 94 as a guide to round off all the corners.

**2** Cut four outer fabric pieces and two wadding/batting pieces measuring 20.5 x 29.25cm (8 x 11½in). Adhere wrong sides together in pairs with wadding/batting in the centre, using spray adhesive. Use your template to round off the two bottom corners of each piece; these are the flaps.

**3** Apply bias binding around the sides and bottom of the two flaps made in step 2.

**4** Take the lining section and place your tools on top in a row. Lay two pieces of elastic over the top, and pin in between each tool. Don't pull the elastic tight.

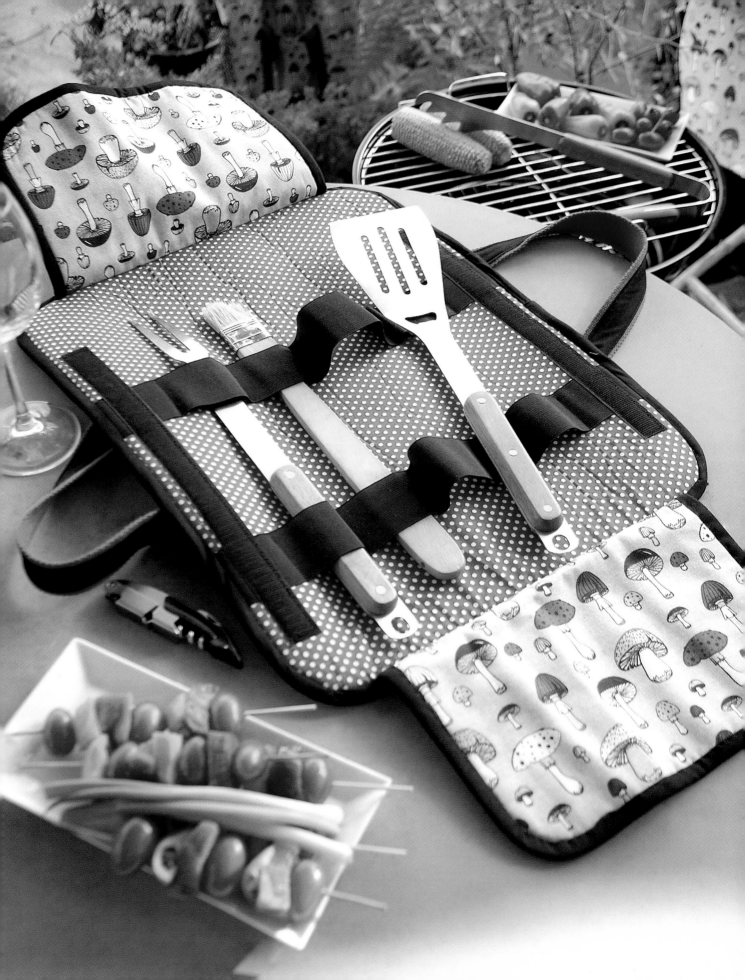

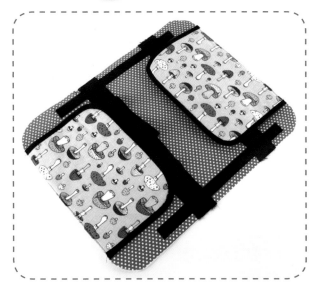

**5** Carefully remove the tools, and sew over the elastic where you've pinned, taking out the pins as you sew. Sew over each end of your stitches a couple of times to strengthen the seam.

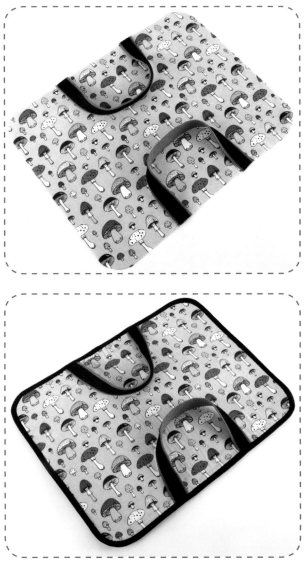

**6** Sew the flaps, facing inwards, to the centre of each short side. Sew the hook-and-loop fastening along the centre of each long side, 2cm (¾in) from the edge.

**7** Take the remaining outer piece, and sew the webbing handles, facing inwards, to each long side, 15.25cm (6in) from the sides. I decorated my webbing by sewing strips of bias binding along the centre.

**8** Adhere the front and back of the roll together, wrong sides facing, with spray adhesive. Apply bias binding all the way round; start with the binding folded, then overlap at the end to make a neat join (see pages 12–13).

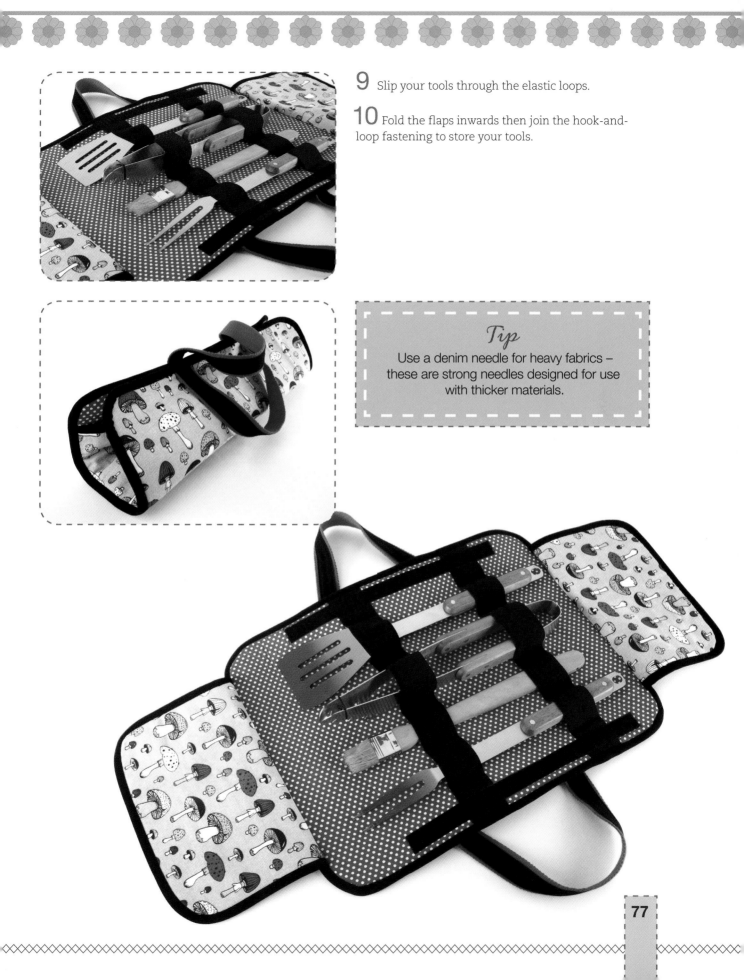

**9** Slip your tools through the elastic loops.

**10** Fold the flaps inwards then join the hook-and-loop fastening to store your tools.

*Tip*
Use a denim needle for heavy fabrics – these are strong needles designed for use with thicker materials.

# BBQ Apron

Pop on this apron when cooking to help protect your clothing from stray sizzles! Denim or canvas is a good fabric choice, and you can easily resize by adding or taking away a little width and length.

## Finished size

56 x 89cm (22 x 35in)

## What you need

97 x 91.5cm (38 x 36in) fabric
3.1m (120in) cotton webbing
3.2m (125in) of 2.5cm (1in) wide bias binding

**1** To make the pocket, cut a rectangle of fabric measuring 38 x 46cm (15 x 18in). Fold in half wrong sides together and sew along each short side, leaving the top open. Snip across the corners.

**2** Turn right side out and press. Apply bias binding across the open edge, folding it over at the ends to make neat.

**3** Cut a piece of fabric for the apron measuring 58.5 x 91.5cm (23 x 36in). Fold in half lengthways and mark 18cm (7in) from the fold along the top of the fabric, then 30.5cm (12in) down the side. Join the two marks and cut to shape the top of the bib.

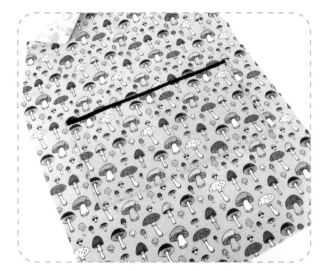

4 Pin the pocket centrally to the front of the apron, 23cm (9in) from the bottom. Sew around the bottom and sides, removing the pins as you sew.

5 Fold in half to crease the centre of the pocket and sew a dividing stitch line if you wish.

6 Cut two strips of fabric measuring 6.5 x 35.5cm (2½ x 14in). Press matching long edges to the wrong side by 5mm (¼in). Press the tops over by 5mm (¼in), then sew. Fold the bottom corners over by 45 degrees to form a triangle at the bottom of each strip. Press.

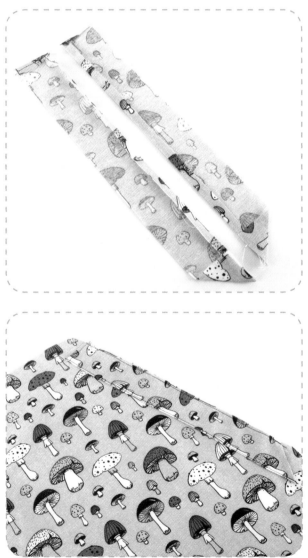

7 Place these two strips over the sides of the apron bib, wrong sides of the strips to the right side of the apron, with the sewn ends at the top and the unfolded edges aligned with the raw edges. Sew along the seam, taking a small seam allowance, then topstitch over the opposite side to make a channel with each strip.

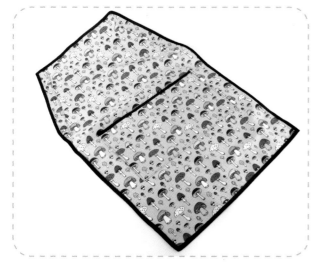

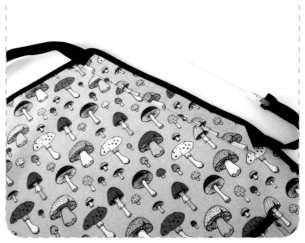

**8** Apply bias binding all around the apron (see pages 12–13).

**9** If you want to, fold over the end of each webbing strip and sew, to protect the ends. Thread it through the bottom of one channel, out of the top and back through the second channel.

**10** Pull the tape so that the tails are even. When you put on the apron, pull the two ends of the tape evenly to fit around the neck. Tie once or twice around the waist.

# Picnic Caddy

This handy caddy is perfect for organizing your picnic plates and cutlery, or would make a useful craft caddy for sewers and knitters! I've made a separate pouch for plates, so that dirty plates aren't placed in the caddy; you might want to make this from oilcloth so that it wipes clean.

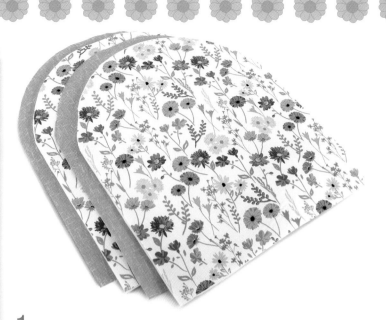

## Finished size

29.25 x 34.25 x 9cm (11½ x 13½ x 3½in)

## What you need

66 x 79cm (26 x 31in) outer fabric

91.5 x 91.5cm (36 x 36in) lining fabric

61 x 61cm (24 x 24in) single-sided fusible foam stabilizer

1.6m (62in) of 2.5cm (1in) wide webbing

91.5cm (36in) of 2.5cm (1in) wide elastic

Magnetic snap fastener

61 x 23cm (24 x 9in) wadding/batting

Repositionable spray fabric adhesive

30.5cm (12in) circle template – I used a plate

1   Cut two outer, two lining and two fusible foam pieces measuring 30.5 x 35.5cm (12 x 14in). Fuse the foam to the wrong sides of the outer fabrics, then use your 30.5cm (12in) circle template to round off the tops of all four pieces.

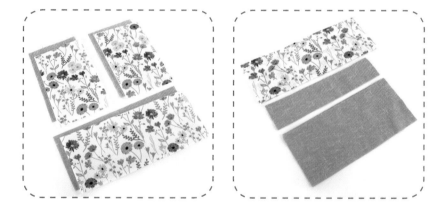

2   Cut one outer, one lining and one foam piece for the base, each measuring 30.5 x 12.75cm (12 x 5in). Cut two outer, two lining and two foam pieces for the sides, each measuring 12.75 x 20.5cm (5 x 8in). Fuse the foam to the wrong sides of the outer pieces.

3   To make the pockets, cut one outer piece measuring 35.5 x 48.25cm (14 x 19in), one lining fabric piece measuring 30.5 x 25.5cm (12 x 10in) and one lining piece measuring 30.5 x 7.5cm (12 x 3in). Fold each piece in half lengthways, right sides together, and sew the long edge to make a tube. Turn right side out and press, then topstitch along the top edges.

4   Sew the sides of the outer fabric pocket to one piece of the caddy lining, 4cm (1½in) up from the bottom; the pocket will be wider than the lining.

**5** Pull the pocket away from the lining, fold both in half and crease the centre of each.

**6** Lay flat again, and sew along the crease line to create two pockets. Make a small pleat in the bottom of each pocket to make them the same width as the lining, then sew across the bottom.

**7** Cut the elastic into three 30.5cm (12in) lengths. Sew two pieces to the remaining caddy lining piece, 9cm (3½in) and 15.25cm (6in) up from the bottom. Sew along the centre of each strip.

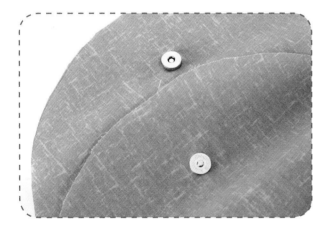

**8** Attach the magnetic snap components to the top of each lining piece, centrally, 5cm (2in) from the top (see page 15).

**9** Cut the webbing in half. Pin to the right sides of each outer caddy piece, 5cm (2in) from the bottom and 9cm (3½in) from each side. Make sure the webbing isn't twisted, then sew in a box shape, stopping 7.5cm (3in) from the top of each panel.

**10** Taking one outer piece, place the wider lining pocket over the bag to cover the ends of the webbing. Sew along the sides and bottom, then down the centre of the pocket, to divide it.

**11** Repeat with the narrow pocket on the second outer caddy piece. Sew the ends of the third elastic piece to either side of the second caddy piece, 7.5cm (3in) above the pocket. Sew seven dividing lines, approximately 4cm (1½in) apart, over both the pocket and elastic. You may wish to vary the distances depending on how you are going to use the caddy. For instance, if you're storing rulers, your pockets may need to be wider.

**12** Sew one long side of the outer end pieces, right sides together, to the caddy.

**13** Sew the end pieces to the remaining outer caddy section to form a 'tube'. Sew in the base panel, matching the corners to the side seams. Start sewing 5mm (¼in) from the corner of the base. You will find it easier to use clips instead of pins to hold the pieces together as the fabric will now be quite thick.

**14** Turn right side out.

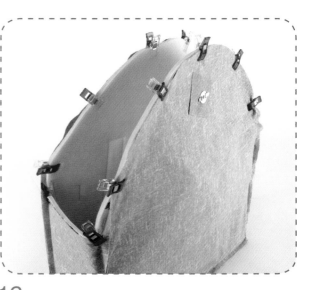

**15** Sew the lining pieces together in the same way, but this time leave a turning gap in one base seam of about 15.25cm (6in).

**16** Drop the outer bag inside the lining, right sides together. Clip around the top, matching the seams.

**17** Sew around the top, removing the clips as you go. Snip into the corners. Turn right side out and sew across the turning gap to close.

**18** Push the lining inside the caddy and press. Topstitch around the top of the caddy.

**19** Make a few hand stitches through both the outer and lining sections in the bottom corners, and at the ends of the elastic pieces, to keep the lining in place.

# The plate pouch

## FOR 23CM (9IN) PLATES

**1** Cut four pieces of lining fabric and two of wadding/batting, each measuring 30.5 x 23cm (12 x 9in). Adhere the wadding/batting to the wrong sides of two pieces with spray adhesive. Cut a 2.5cm (1in) square from the bottom two corners of each piece.

**2** Sew the tops of the padded (outer) pieces right sides together to the unpadded (lining) pieces.

**3** Place the two sections right sides together, matching outer to outer and lining to lining, and sew all the way round, leaving the corners unsewn and leaving a turning gap in the base seam of the lining pieces of about 10cm (4in). Pinch the cut-out corners so that the side seams sit over the base seams, and sew to make the pouch bottom square.

**4** Turn right side out and sew the opening closed.

**5** Push the lining inside the pouch and press. Topstitch around the opening to complete.

# Buttoned Seat Pad

Buttons add a great finishing touch to this seat pad; I used mismatched buttons for a quirky look! Bear in mind that you won't be able to remove the cover for laundering, so you may wish to give the pad a spray of fabric protector to help keep it clean.

## Finished size

41 x 38 x 4cm (16 x 15 x 1½in); my seat measures 41 x 38 (16 x 15in)

## What you need

46 x 46cm (18 x 18in) piece of 4cm (1½in) thick foam
102 x 51cm (40 x 20in) fabric
Four buttons
Embroidery thread and a long needle

**1** Make a pattern for your seat using the same method as on page 28. Cut the foam to size.

**2** Cut two pieces of fabric 2.5cm (1in) larger all the way round than your pattern.

**3** Sew, right sides together, leaving a turning gap along the back edge of the pad. Snip into the curved seams with pinking shears.

**4** Turn right side out. Push the foam pad inside the cover. Hand sew the opening closed using ladder stitch (see page 10).

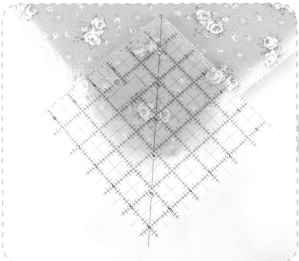

5 Measure and mark 11.5cm (4½in) from each corner.

6 With your long needle and embroidery thread, sew a button over each of these marks, taking the needle back and forth through all the layers and knotting the thread on top of the buttons to finish.

# Bottle Tote

Arrive in style at the BBQ with this useful twin bottle holder with handy corkscrew pocket! Make sure you choose strong fabric and sew the handles on securely, as the tote will have to carry a fair amount of weight.

## *Finished size*

38 x 27 x 9cm
(15 x 10½ x 3½in)

## *What you need*

86.5 x 33cm (34 x 13in)
outer fabric

86.5 x 33cm (34 x 13in)
single-sided fusible
foam stabilizer

99.5 x 33cm (39 x 13in)
lining fabric

1.8m (70in) of 2.5cm (1in)
wide webbing

1.1m (40in) of 2.5cm (1in)
wide bias binding

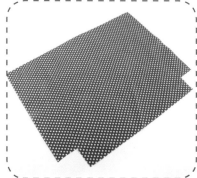

**1** Cut two outer pieces, each measuring 43.25 x 33cm (17 x 13in). Fuse the stabilizer to the wrong sides. Cut away a 5cm (2in) square from each bottom corner.

**2** Cut two lining pieces the same.

**3** Cut your webbing in half. Pin each end to the base of one tote outer piece, 7.5cm (3in) from the cut-out corners. Make sure the handles are straight, then sew in a box shape, finishing 10cm (4in) from the top of the tote. Repeat for the other side of the tote.

**4** Cut a piece of lining fabric measuring 12.75 x 23cm (5 x 9in) for the corkscrew pocket. Fold in half wrong sides together and sew along the side seams, leaving the top open. Snip across the corners. Turn right side out and press. Apply bias binding across the open top of the pocket, folding the edges under to make neat.

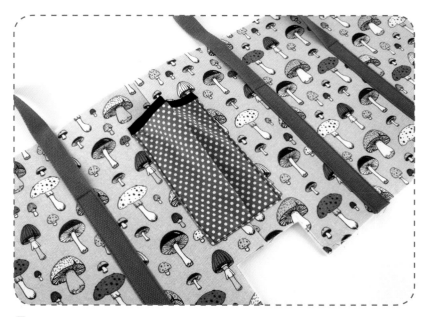

**5** Place the two outer pieces right sides together and sew along one side. Open out and pin the pocket over the seam, 5cm (2in) from the top. Make a small pleat in the bottom to reduce the width of the pocket to 10cm (4in). Sew around the sides and bottom of the pocket.

**6** Fold the tote right sides together and sew the remaining side and base seams, leaving the cut-out corners unsewn. Pinch the side and base seams together and then sew across the cut-out corners to make the base square. Turn right side out.

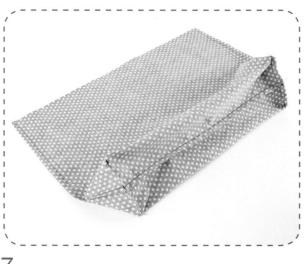

**7** Sew the lining pieces together in the same way.

**8** Drop the lining inside the outer with wrong sides facing and the seams matching. Use fabric clips to hold the two sections together. You'll find clips easier than pins as the foam is quite thick.

**9** Sew around the top, close to the raw edge. Apply bias binding around the top of the tote (see pages 12–13).

**10** Draw a 2.5 x 5cm (1 x 2in) box shape in between the handles on one side of the tote, centrally, 6.5cm (2½in) from the top. Sew around this box through both sides of the tote to create a divider.

*Your pockets are large enough to carry a couple of bottles of wine or soft drinks!*

# Templates

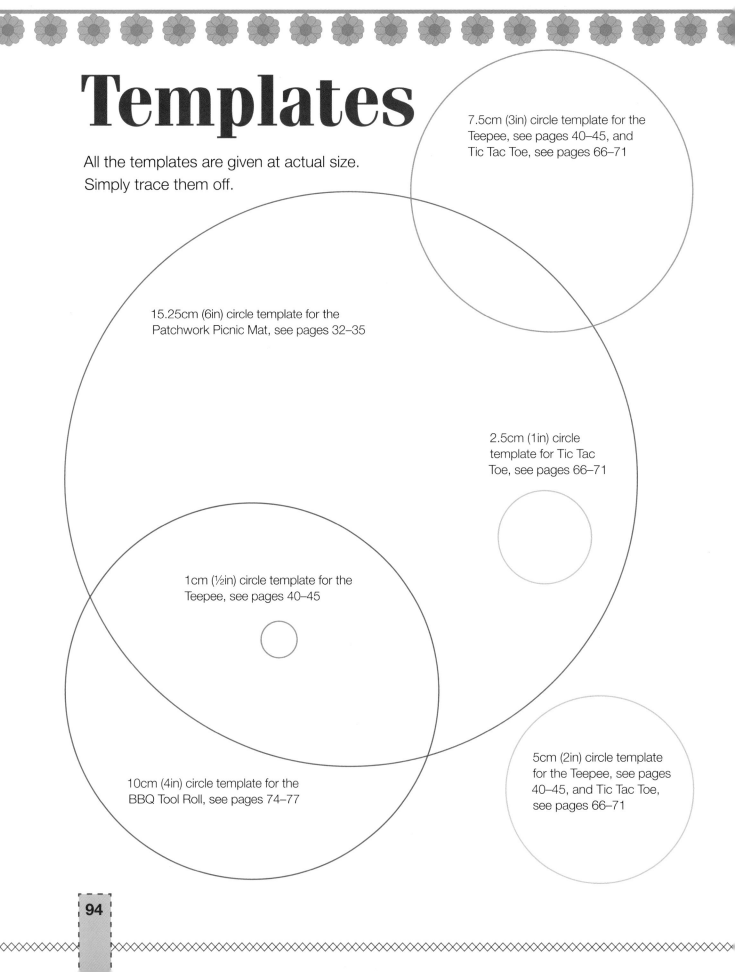

All the templates are given at actual size.
Simply trace them off.

7.5cm (3in) circle template for the
Teepee, see pages 40–45, and
Tic Tac Toe, see pages 66–71

15.25cm (6in) circle template for the
Patchwork Picnic Mat, see pages 32–35

2.5cm (1in) circle
template for Tic Tac
Toe, see pages 66–71

1cm (½in) circle template for the
Teepee, see pages 40–45

10cm (4in) circle template for the
BBQ Tool Roll, see pages 74–77

5cm (2in) circle template
for the Teepee, see pages
40–45, and Tic Tac Toe,
see pages 66–71

Insect wings template for Tic Tac Toe,
see pages 66–71

Heart template for the Reverse Appliqué
Placemat, see pages 18–21, and the
Heart Decorations, see pages 48–49

Heart templates for the Rustic Table
Accessories, see pages 62–65

# Index